Musings
Love and Life

Musings
Love and Life

POEMS WRITTEN AND EDITED
BY MIKE SUTCLIFFE

First paperback edition April 2020

Jacket photograph by David Johnson at maxblackphotos.com

ISBN 978-1-8380206-0-6

Published by Michael R.H. Sutcliffe
Mike.sutcliffe1@btinternet.com

CONTENTS

MUSINGS

FOREWORD

Having been raised amongst the moorlands of rural
Yorkshire, I have always had my eyes open to the
beauty of nature surrounding us and the normal folk,
who are the subject of many of my poems, often with
a sense of wonder. There have been many influences
across the years, most notably the paradigm shift I
experienced with the birth of my children, an event
that took my understanding of unconditional love to a
new level.

In later life, I have been fortunate to have had the
opportunity of travelling extensively; experiencing
many different cultures, giving me a broad outlook on
the lives of others, yet my heart will always lie in my
beloved Yorkshire Dales. Through my journey of life it
has come to represent a place of deep spirituality,
where I can let my soul and imagination run free.

Having always been a keen observer of the human
psyche and the effects that everyday life has upon us,
I have drawn on these experiences and translated
them into poetry that I would describe as 'rustic', in
that my poems come straight from my heart and have
a passionate, earthy feel to them, enticing the reader
to visualise the story being told through the use of
strong imagery.

Not adhering to a particular style, this collection of
poems should be read as a story from start to finish.
In only a few, short words and stanzas, it is possible
to create a story of true depth and meaning.

With poetic influences ranging from the great Beat
Poets of post World War II, through to the classics
such as Tennyson and Thomas Hardy, readers will find
an interesting and diverse mix of styles and topics to
entertain, from the very first page.

Musings

LAY DOWN YOUR GUNS

Wars and crusades, all fought in His name,
They think They are sane, to kill in His name.
But it won't bring change, it's completely in vain,
just bystanders slain, and the lucky ones maimed.

Muslims and Christians, Gentiles and Jews,
to whom You call God, is Your right to choose.
Be it; Buddha or Allah, Elohim or God,
whatever you call Him,
killing is not
what God was meant to mean, no bombs on the
streets.
For innocence lost, is not about God.

To temples, and mosques, and churches You flee,
to worship and pray, with such love, and glee.
For He; You kneel, You pray, and You heed,
taking His words
as You want them to be, ignoring what they,
should really mean.

Lay down Your guns, and Your arms, and Your bombs,
for Your bigoted hatred, will win over none,
just leave You alone, at the foot of His throne.

For the way that We live, for Us and for Me,
should be in peace; alive, safe and free.
So lay down Your guns, please let it be,
lay down Your guns, and let Us,
live in peace.

THE LONELY TREE

Have you sat under The Lonely Tree,
taken a moment, had a day dream?

Did you ever look, pause for a while,
musing his past, did it make you smile?

A whole life spent, weathering storms,
crooked and bent, slightly deformed.

Scarred and worn, bark partly eaten,
standing up proud, still never beaten.

What of the others, where have they gone?
Once there were many, now just one.

Long it had been, since friend or foe seen,
so long it had been, for The Lonely Tree.

If you are passing, just stop a short while,
pay your respects, it may make him smile.

As time goes by, for you and for me,
we all will become, The Lonely Tree.

WHY AM I?

Why am I, and
will I always be?
Springtime melting snow
or, an eternal
ocean sea?

Where to wander, and
dare I dream?
Will my path
meander, like
a gentle mountain stream?

How to live, and
what to be?
The heaven bound
angel or, the devil's
carnal scream?

What was my life, and
did I really see?
Was it simple in its
beauty, in its
love for me?

When is the end, and
what will it be?
A sentence for the
executioner, to
finally set me free?

Who will remember, and
why will that be?
Words fading on
a page until, I
never was me?

ECHOES OF SOULS

Listen to the wind, whispers in the leaves,
all around are signs; in the Earth, in the trees.

Playing in the clouds, shadows passing by,
forgotten long ago, glimpses with an eye.

Searching for the lost, those never to be found,
departed in their grief, their song a haunting sound.

Eternities of drifting, upon our corporeal plain,
their hunger to move on, will always be in vain.

Now your mind is open, tuned in to their cries,
you can hear them calling, so lonely in the night.

Please never forget, this secret that you hold,
you are now a guardian, for the echoes of souls.

WHAT OF MEMORIES

---

do they fade as the setting sun
over lost horizons where darkness lurks
shrouding their meaning
in the mists of time passed

to be lost in eternity

do they hide as the child's twighlight dreams
shielded from fears
glimpsed through a fading nights light
their touch
teasing the minds straining reach

with never ending distance

do they live as the rainbows fleeting visit
a passing moment
whose colours flash bright beauty's smile
one single moment of wonder

to fade in the gathering storms wake

do they roam as the free spirit
drifting in the minds eye
whose spark lights life
not night
for the joy of what was

to delight in the smiles of remembrance

THE POETS TREE

Sometimes I sit beneath The Poets Tree,
where legends linger, not yet me.
Their passage earned, with words so pure,
their names etched in, their place assured.

Byron, Tennyson, Burns and Poe,
I feel their words course through my soul.
They bring me comfort, when I am alone,
lost in my mind, where poems grow.

Breathing deep, their scent floods in,
my senses ache from deep within,
of powerful imagery, rhythm and rhyme,
lost in their words from another time.

If I dare to look up, then perhaps I will see,
a new green shoot, that may one day be me.

STARLIGHT SANCTUARY

The dew damp dawn calls an ending to the night,
the first bird song, a tolling bell, a call to flight.
Some now wake, some now sleep, all follow nature's
lore,
the hidden starlight sanctuary, shelters from the
waking dawn.

The stoic sun, as ancient oak, whose eyes belie its
stare,
gazes down upon the battlefield, of war in Poseidon's
lair.
Mermaids flight, dolphins fight, ashore the unicorns
run,
all seek the starlight sanctuary, veiled from the raging
sun.

The axe now rests, its work is done, the fire burning
bright,
tall tales are told, no truths unfold, beneath the fading
light.
Through glinting eyes, shrouded by the night, a secret
to remain,
for the hidden starlight sanctuary, all will look in vain.

Embers fade, ash fresh made, the blood red moon
above,
searching for the starlight sanctuary, its forever secret
love.

BEANUTY

---

are you blinded
perfume
makeup
bodies taught

what are they
self important
mere features
no more

where do I look
your smile
perfect skin
look past

do you see
deeper
with your eyes
the beauty within

A COMPLICATED MAN

There are too many halves to make just one whole,
they fight for supremacy, they tear at my soul,
for the right to be free, to escape from within,
to be the dominant one, the one that must win.

There is carefree and happy, so light in its mood,
mixed with laughter and joy, bringing all that is good.
But then there is thoughtful, it is deep and sad,
raising anger and fury, it is boiling and mad.

Still there is more, dwelling deep down inside,
there is love and romance, that so often hides.
But not ruthless and cold, with the harshest of stares,
that is daring and bold, it never really cares.

Which one today, that is out of my hands,
it was once said to me, that I am a complicated man.

SMOKE FILLED ROOMS

---

drifting murky
smoke filled rooms
with rickety chairs
and full bar stools
crushed out ash
and empty glasses
strangers glance
but that soon passes

alone they sit
with all the others
pondering lives
of long lost lovers
faded images
what could have been
a life once glimpsed
but never seen

ageing music
sawdust floors
rattling hinges
on worn out doors
block the way
to free themselves
keeping them there
to live out hell

drifting deep
in nicotine and liquor
nearly gone
from now forever
a desperate sight
these disparate souls
forever lost
and broken and old

IF I WERE ~ PART 1

If I were a bird ~
my aloofness in nobility
soaring
on the grace of heavens breath
with wings lent by angels

If I were a whale ~
my solitude sung in song
wandering
far across the ancient seas
with a speed of timeless wisdom

If I were a lion ~
my mane the crown of kings
roaming
through scorched savannah lands
with a roar of regal dignity

If I were a man ~
my senses dulled by progress
humbled
by the insignificance of cities
with sadness at my arrogance

IF I WERE ~ PART 2

If I were a bird
soaring high up in the sky
I would watch the world beneath
see the people and their lies

If I were a whale
wandering seas and oceans deep
I would hide beneath the waves
for my safety I must keep

If I were a lion
roaming through my vast kingdom
I would cower at their guns
until the hunters were all gone

If I were a man
with the world beneath my feet
I would rape it for myself
it is mine for me to keep

A GLIMPSE

there is life all around him
gleaming
teaming
his eyes open in wonder
a bird
a snail
a butterfly
innocence shines in his smile
in his eyes
he looks on
just watching
not daring to move

is he a part of this
nature at work
he stands and wonders
in his awe and naivety
they told him of God
is this his doing
it cannot be
there must be much more

it is living
connected
moving as one
vibrant and flowing
vast and great
is this the first time
he has opened his eyes
suddenly so small
not tall

mother is calling him
breaking the spell
slowly
slowly
he retreats from this place
he has glimpsed for a moment
looking within

time for tea now
turn the TV on

THE TURNING OF A PAGE

Brilliantly sparkling high up in the sky,
have you ever stopped and wondered;
why?

The specks are in the distance; far, far away,
we see them in the night, they fall asleep by day.

Children look in wonder, so many suns above,
for all it should be magical, like everlasting love.

Some think it must be only us, that we are all alone,
they see our Earth as everything, not just a tiny stone.

History was written, by man for all our age,
still not even a chapter, just the turning of a page.

Time stretches back forever, so far it is not seen,
our minds too small to comprehend; just what does it
mean?

Now look at the sky, in the darkness of the night,
see beyond the twinkles, the glinting of the light.

Are you looking deeper, the beauty way up high?
Can you see the wonder, where galaxies collide?

Do you see how small we are, how big the Universe?
We are merely one so small, where all else is diverse.

When man is gone and Earth remains, what else will
there be? The stars still glowing loud and bright, for
others still to see.

WHAT IS HAPPINESS?

What is happiness, I have often wondered,
is it inside us, or just an object to be plundered?

There is many a thing to make us smile,
for each it is different, yet for all worthwhile.

We judge by our standards those in our lives,
by our own paradigm, we see through our eyes.

They talk of a shift, but can it be real,
or is it for others, for those whom we feel?

Do they need us, to be how they see,
or can they let us, be us, for me?

That is a question we should always ask,
it is part of the test, one of the tasks.

For if I am me, I am all that they see,
is that enough, it really should be?

You should be you, is all that I can ask,
if that is the case, then your happiness will last.

THE AGE OF AUSTERITY

No money, no cash, no readies to flash,
as the rent man calls round, if I don't pay,
he will hound,
until he has his flesh, and, well, you know the rest.

Broke and alone, all I have is my home,
no food on the shelves, just a gnawed,
broken bone,
of the meat from last week, it was all I could eat,
as I look in my fridge, nothing left,
just some cheese and no money to flash,
to pay for a cab, to get me from here.
So I stay, in my fear,
right here with my tears,
wishing I wasn't here.

Broke, so broke me, what I'd give for a penny,
but no chance of that, I must live,
without cash.

Look out the window, it's raining, again,
where did the sun go?
When will it return?
To bring back some light,
to my dark and dull life,
that leaves me apart from the rest of the World;
no money, no wife, just a sad,
dreary life.

I watch them walk by,
with their heads bowed down,
living like me, with no smile, just a frown,
at the state of my life; no money, no wife,
waiting for it, to come my way again,
waiting for it,
to break through the never ending rain.

Wishing my life would once more begin,
as I live in the now; no money ,no cash.
My life is now over, just look at the past,
when I had money, and I had cash,
but it didn't last, so I live in the past,
I know that will last.

The age of prosperity, overrun by austerity,
so that we end up broke,
for all of eternity.

The End!

TOMORROW

If it were tomorrow, what came before?
My life skipped a beat, that day is no more.

Where did I go, and what did I see?
Was it a good day, a good one for me?

If I were to wish, for each day to pass,
looking ahead, please go fast.

Tomorrow is the new, today is the old,
I may pawn it away, my memories sold.

If it were tomorrow, today left behind,
was it in vain, was I cruel, or kind?

Would I be poorer, with yesterday gone,
or simply oblivious, to all I had done?

If I were to wish, what would it be,
the loss of today, with no memory?

Imagine it now, such a beautiful day,
each must be cherished, never wished away.

MY OLD GRANDFATHER CLOCK

Tick tock, tick tock, my old grandfather clock,
whose face ever changes, yet still stays the same.
His hands are relentless, ornate and yet plain,
guiding the way through the night, to the day.

Tick tock, tick tock, my old grandfather clock,
whose chimes bring the signs, and the changing of
time,
keeping me true, with his relentless rhyme,
his stoic dignity, bathed in serenity for all of eternity.

Tick tock, tick tock, my old grandfather clock,
whose strong brass chains, still bear the weights.
Each swing of the pendulum, never being late,
just the movement of time, showing on his face.

Tick tock, tick tock, my old grandfather clock,
whose constancy keeps me, wrapped in his safety.

THE BELLS

Ring ring, ring ring ~ as the worshipers sing,
their prayers flow upward to places
where nobody goes, or knows, perhaps not even Him.

Yet the virgins call. Which He is He, wherever You may
be?

What need pervades an existence, with such insanity,
that Their crutch lies in a Heaven, to be given to the
non-existent other,
who shadows Their lives, where eyes close to all of
life's beauty,
conforming only to the ancient word's page,
ignoring today,
and whose name is many.

Ring ring, ring ring ~ as They sing to Him.

Who shines so bright with words that light life, with
delight,
yet whose own eyes close to the reality of life,
where prayers go unheard in Our ethereal existence?

Why?

Stand at Your own alter,
where destiny serves a purpose, not defined or
confined
by His words, don't falter.

Ring ring, ring ring ~ to Your own song You must sing.

LIVE FOR TODAY

Loans and overdraughts, taxes and greed,
all of it comes, in a credit squeeze.
When we need, yes need, to let go of greed,
it won't let us go, it just fuels
and feeds.

When will it end, how long will it last?
Is the crunch here forever, devoid of cash?
To last so long in a world of crass people,
who will last, I can guarantee that,
lending their cash.

Living on empty, looking around,
at the sound, yes the sound, of a valueless pound.
The price to be fed, when you're in the red,
not even enough,
for a loaf of bread.

Live for today, that is all you can do,
for today is now, in solitary mood,
where tomorrow is made of; if, maybe, when.
So live in the now, forget about then,
which is all about them, and the money
they lent.

FACELESS NAMES

Faceless names playing political games, for their own gains,
they preach change, to us, the people, so dumb they must think,
not rich
~ such stink.

Liberals, conservatives, neo-fascists, the loony left merging
into grey suited masses, of image consultants and speech writers,
all with back stage passes
~ to power.

At a price, or for more, yes for more, for me, please give ME more.

His fault, her fault, but never was it mine.
See which way I point, see my smile so bright, when I grin,
you catch the shine
~ of elitism.

Corruption and starvation, no jobs for all the nation,
are today's anthologies,
sung high up from the roof tops, of the smoking chimney
working classes.
You ungrateful mob, just apologise, for now we rise, to power so high
~ stay down.

No heat, no fuel, a gluttony of exam passes,
don't the stats look good?
Now forget about the floods, and the hunger,
all is good
~ for you small people, so good, such luck.

The stench of power and money and greed,
for all of the warnings, the public should heed
~ what changes?

Just the names ~ without faces ~ in powerful places.

THE OLD BUS STOP

Life stands still at the old bus stop,
where the gangs roam free, no police,
the cops,
too scared to go there with them;
the scavengers, thieves,
and the whores with men.

Don't dare to go, leave them be,
they can fend for themselves,
if they die,
who will see; not them, not you,
not me will see.
They are nothing.

Tattooed bodies roam the streets,
with guns, and drugs, giving out sweets,
to seduce the young,
give them a gun, they are theirs forever,
they are part of the gang,
to die,
perhaps,
to die with a bang,
however they die who will give a damn,
they were just another,
one of a gang.

See the graffiti adorning the walls,
of the old bus stop in the middle of wars,
of rivals, and thugs, with their knives they mug,
the innocent few who never knew,
not to go after dark, or before the lark,
to the old bus stop,
just next to the park.

NOTHING IN PARTICULAR

I was thinking about nothing, nothing in particular,
well, perhaps, it might just be something, but what
was it?

It escapes me now, as my mind's electrics fire in
spasms of who knows what,
to places of fortitude, where peace sometimes sleeps.

Maybe it was something, something vexing,
of importance, and need, and desire, that should be in
my mind, right now,
for its own self importance and idealism conforming,
to their points of view.

Or something just like that.

Or maybe just nothing, nothing of importance,
maybe just blank, white sheets of me canvass.

Is blank allowed in such swirling times and minds of
distinction,
so ordinary, with the stresses of life that eat at the
news?

Maybe, who knows, do you?

It was nothing in particular, I think,
I'm not yet certain, but I will ponder some more,
to myself.

It may be of merit and worth more, more of my
consideration,
where time stops still on the fells, as I walk in silence,
pondering life and all eternity's meanings in the air,
and the wind,
without papers, or reporters, or them.

But probably not, perhaps just nothing, nothing in
particular.

Love

TO CATCH A SNOWFLAKE

Bathed by the moonlight and the sparkling distant
stars,
where ancient lovers live, their aura seeping from afar.
As the first fall flows, diamond crystals coat the
ground,
in their symphony of silence, a crashing nothingness of
sound.

Fragile, frozen touches, brush against reluctant minds,
the warmth in their beauty, sending shivers down the
spine.
Eager hands reach out, grasping harshly, closing tight,
the frenzied fury of their need, ending each one's life.

For the briefest of moments, their grace is sublime,
yet in an instant they are gone, like the passage of
time.
To catch a falling snowflake, stop and wonder how,
with no past and no future, they exist in the now.

If the time should come, if your soul begins to calm,
you may look at your own snowflake, resting gently on
your palm.

IF WE GET THERE

We already have our day at the beach,
locked in our memory, forever in reach.
We talked, we laughed, we smiled, we kissed,
I was lost in your soul, drawn into your mist.

Some beautiful moments, our very own song,
wrapped in my arms, as we became one.
I held your hand tight, I will never let go,
you are part of me now, making me whole.

If we get there, let's make our list,
let's live it together, let's end with a kiss.
Each day must be ours, we will live them together,
making every new day, the start of forever.

When we get there, our love bright and strong,
for the rest of our lives, we will be one.

NOW WE ARE THERE

If we get there, seems so long ago,
for such a short journey, a twisting long road.
There were smiles and laughter, illness and tears,
yet we conquered them all, forged with love from our
fears.

You have stood by my side, through the dark and the
night,
your love is always with me, a beacon of light.
I give you the same, and I promise you this;
a lifetime of love, and support, as my gift.

Now we are there, we are making our list,
we live life together, end each day with a kiss.
The future is ours, to be lived together,
for every new day, is our start of forever.

Now we are there, you are the love of my life,
it makes me complete, to call you my wife.

THE BEACH

Fading over the eternal horizon,
to dance in far off playgrounds.
Auburn flames sear outward,
fighting the days near end.

Rolling from the white horses manes,
the touch of Poseidon's breath
paints lips with drifting, salty air.

Lost in the ebb of moon pulled tides,
no words break the crashing silence.

Our hands mingle.

TELL HER

---

tell her I will wait
under our old oak tree
my mind will be wandering
my spirit will be free
she will float in my dreams
she will whisper my name
in my mind she is there
in my soul she remains

tell her I miss her
in the long lonely nights
cold on my own
without her by my side
no warmth on my body
no breath on my face
where she used to lie
with such beauty and grace

tell her I live
just one day at a time
that my world has been empty
no rhythm or rhyme
when she left it was day
but since then it is night
if I close my eyes tight
she comes back to my life

tell her I am waiting
I know she will come
back to her home
no longer alone
her spirit was freed
she crossed over the line
I pray that one day
she will once again be mine

WHISPERS OF ESSENCE

---

loves breath whispers to your essence
as a feather gently glancing the soul
~ to linger a while

intertwined streams of emotion seep inward
penetrating solitude's opaque view
~ raising hopes anew

tacit truths are shared within one glance
mingling as the colours of a palette
~ laid on fresh canvass

naked within your all encompassing safety
accepting like the fragile child's trust
~ given to you

OUR SUMMER

Do you remember the start of forever,
our summer of love, we lived it together?
The hopes and the dreams, so much to do,
from the moment we met, I gave me to you.

Do you remember the sand at our feet,
the theatre in Minnack, our first New Years Eve?
The fireworks went up in the Lands End sky,
I knew in that moment, as I looked into your eyes.

Do you remember, it was a beautiful night,
I said that I love you, I held your hand tight?
With diamonds and sapphires, forged from the moon,
it was made with my heart, with my love for you.

Always remember, for the rest of our lives,
that you are my summer, the love of my life.

ODE TO SHAME

I walked along the path
sometimes left and sometimes right
I did not know the way
yet I could see a distant light

I thought about the end
and what that would mean for me
I stared so long and hard
but somehow I could not see

I strained to know the way
as my mind was filled with pain
for my short and lonely life
so much anger and such shame

it was that thing still haunting me
for which my punishment should last
all my sins along the way
I felt should hurt and be so harsh

on the day you came to me
when you looked into my eyes
you healed me with your love
your faith devotion and your pride

TRUE LOVE'S KISS

New found depths, that grip me there,
her subtle scent, drifts through the air.
Consuming me, with passionate rage,
we are bound forever, I am her slave.

Melting together, becoming one,
our bodies symmetry, a single tone.
Please linger still, I must savour all,
to capture her, within my soul.

Drifting now, all time has stopped,
our inhibitions, have all been lost.
A swirling maelstrom, of carnal pleasure,
I sip from the cup, of her deepest treasure.

The possibilities become limitless,
when you've tasted the lips, of true love's kiss.

A BRIGHTER DAY

---

when you wake to the lark
and the day seems dark
think of the light
then watch its flight
as it wings on its way
it will brighten your day

when you feel all alone
vulnerable and prone
think of me then
like the song of a wren
always for you
with my love ever true

VIENNA

---

those few moments
do you recall
we lived in love
I consumed you all

you held my hand
lost in your eyes
the moment took us
just truth ~ no lies

our love as deep
as it can be
you breathed me in
and made me see

we lived a dream
a life together
blinking our eyes
in our Vienna

how time mocked
so wrong for us
we tried so hard
yet ended lost

we should have been
just us forever
in our beautiful city
Wien, Vienna

now I've lost you
my heart still trembles
you live within me
I am forever humbled

you were mine
and now it's never
the love we shared
is gone forever

yet in my heart
we will always be
in our Vienna
just you and me

INSIDE THE WALLS

---

inside my mind
where the Worlds collide
there is chaos not order
where all is alive

it is so random
no order to be had
but the smile on my face
tells a story not sad

some see me complex
a web and a maze
living my life
in a dream and a haze

they try to get in me
just for a while
I sit back and watch them
behind my closed smile

I peak through my walls
as they try to get in
they batter and hammer
believing they are thin

but they are so tall
so thick and so strong
they cannot get through them
and see this as wrong

but you yes you
you melted them away
for you they are open
in the night and the day

from the moment I saw you
the walls all tumbled
no barriers to you
in your presence I am humbled

my deepest of secrets
to you I have told
I gave them with trust
I knew you would hold

my past is unravelled
you now know it all
I know you will love me
and not let me fall

my walls are still there
for all else to see
but you are behind them
inside with me

you know me, you have me
all that I am
I give myself completely
I am now in your hands

THE AGONY OF TIME

---

her words gentle in their tone
whose softness pervade my soul
with the consuming scent
~ of she

lost in the depths of her heart
whose comfort speed it away
forgotten in the rush
~ of ecstasy

wrapped in a symbiotic womb
whose bubble of time releases
snapped from the fantasy
~ of us

cold awakening to the closing door
whose echo is amplified
by the emptiness and solitude
~ of reality

watching the tick of each hand
whose passing now taunts me
slowed by the agony
~ of waiting

THE CONNECTION

---

beep beep, beep beep
goes my text coming in
when I'm just pressing send
yes we did it again
it's our pattern you see
being one
her and me

way back in time
when my thoughts were just mine
I really couldn't see
what she would truly mean
that this love could be
so real
for me

it may take it's time
that love most don't find
but one day it will rhyme
as you merge into one
with each others thoughts
playing just a single tone

this connection we found
after years milling around
until fate intervened
and made us
it seems,
finally be
we

DO YOU ADORE

Do you lie there in the night,
in awe but not in fright?
Do you look through squinting eyes,
smile inwardly with pride?

If you breathe the spell may go,
like the quickly thawing snow.
If you blink they may be gone,
in a second there is none.

When you drift into your dreams,
can you know just what it means?
When you see them in your sleep,
that you are theirs to keep.

Will you wake up in the dawn,
with a smile not just a yawn?
Will you dare look to your side,
filled up with love and pride?

FATE

what's meant to be
won't pass you by
if it really should be
it will be in your life

looking too hard
in depths of the night
reading the cards
in the gentle lamp light

the harder it feels
the more you are sad
it won't make it real
just make you more mad

don't look for it here
don't look for it there
it will play on your fear
it will make your heart tear

one day it will come
of that you will see
no longer alone
if it is meant to be

TRUE LOVE

---

as I drift into sleep
she is there in my mind
as the darkness takes hold
it is my hand she finds

when I wake to the dawn
she may not be with me
yet inside my heart
it is her that I see

when I feel her touch
like a shimmering glance
my body begins to tremble
my heart starts to dance

as she holds me so tight
wrapped up in her arms
I feel safety and warmth
far away from all harm

for years in my prison
I believed I was free
with somebody else
yet really just me

I thought that I knew
how it felt deep inside
I now know the truth
until you I would hide

my life is complete
you brought that to me
stay with me forever
let true love really be

I WAIT

I wait
why
it taunts me
laughter echoes
baiting my anticipation
as time passes
slowly
too slowly

I wait
for eternity
to come
for me
not yet
it slows
almost stopping
with a sneer

I wait
mind playing
paranoia growing
like a cancer
nightmares spiral
not knowing when
she
will come

I wait

A LOST SOUL FOUND

Drifting through time, alone and shutdown,
the World all around me, just passed with a frown.
I watched from the outside, lives meandering through,
their turbulent turmoil, none of which I knew.

For too many years, I was safe behind walls,
away from the madness, the fights and the wars.
For when it all ended, relief touched me deep,
four years in my slumber, away and asleep.

No thoughts of finding, a love that was lost,
it was never really real, just a memory past.
Happy in my solitude; my fun and my play,
the last thing I thought, that *it* would come my way.

Suddenly you were there, shining and bright,
I immediately awoke, and came back to the light.
My heart skipped a beat, when I gazed upon you,
such an amazing person; strong, beautiful and true.

Now every day, I am awake and alive,
I take a deep breath, at the happiness in my life.
You enter my thoughts, as my eyes open wide,
the first and the last, in the day and the night.

You have found me and made me, you are my World,
we will melt our lives together, just a boy and a girl.
So thank you sweet lady, for being with me,
you have made me complete, for all eternity.

THE LITTLE THINGS

---

it's the little things you see
like making my tea
it just shows she cares
that she's thinking of me

what else could I ask
nothing but a meal
just the thought that I'm here
that's what makes it real

some can do flash
throw their money around, so crass
but I don't want that
I know it won't last

just the simplest of things
bring a smile deep inside
always thinking of her
she's something worthwhile

I miss her you know
when she's busy and away
but I know that's alright
she'll be back another day

a house, cat and Mum
kids and a job
she has her hands full
with that crazy lot

but she still finds the time
amongst all of the rest
for the thoughtful things
they are the best

it's the little things you see
that make a person see
just how much she cares
and loves me, for me

UNCONDITIONAL LOVE

---

it is as deep as it can be
when I look into their eyes
I see them with a smile
I see myself inside

what is this magic
that brought them to me
so perfect in every way
how can it be

how were they made
I wonder in awe
it was me and her
but there must be more

such perfection I see
so there has to be
so much more than just us
so much more than just me

when they look at me
it is all they can see
I see it in their eyes
their love for me

I smell them and watch them
growing so tall
I pick them back up
and never let them fall

it is simple and honest
straightforward no more
the love of your child
is the World, it is all

for they are my future
my hope and my life
I will love and protect them
to the day that I die

EXCITEMENT

---

what makes me tingle
and jingle inside
making me spin
almost bursting within

rising up high
like the brand new tide
welling from deep
so that I cannot speak

eyes open wide
in the middle of the night
it keeps me awake
so that sleep cannot take

then it is time
for it to be mine
I am exploding with fun
my excitement has won

NO LONGER ALONE

---

so long alone
in the days when she's gone
so long alone
waiting patiently at home

I watch the sun rise
from my opaque window
I watch the sun rise
when she's back I don't know

the morning dew sparkles
with spring time in bloom
the morning dew sparkles
under a sleeping moon

the warmth of the sun
feels so gentle on my face
the warmth of the sun
is mine alone to face

the sun sets to sleep
at the end of the day
the sun sets to sleep
leaving just me to play

now she is back
she takes hold of me
now she is back
I will never let her leave

THE RIDE

---

up and down
round and round
sometimes a smile
sometimes a frown
always with thought
deep in the head
the heart plays the tune
the rest of it led

when it is up
it is easy for all
when it is down
so many fall
they stumble and trip
then let it all go
forgetting the truth
when times feel low

they are the ones
without love deep inside
they are the ones
who jump off the ride
in it for them
forgetting all others
not really true
simply just lovers

then there are those
who deep down inside
stand up and fight
refusing to hide
in it forever
supporting their lover
in it for them
for us and each other

THE START OF FOREVER

how did it happen
the start of forever
I closed my eyes tight
thinking of never

one at a time
my days passed me by
the past still with me
living the lie

it felt like a dream
I did not know why
I must be asleep
my eyes so tight

I woke from my slumber
you lay by my side
a vision appeared
my eyes opened wide

as time passed by
I finally could see
that forever was real
it had started for me

FOR LOVE

---

she fills me
consumes me
eats me with her being
she flows herself around me
in my waking dreams

my aura is surrounded
merged into one soul
my body melts into her
I will never be
alone

when I am not with her
feeling empty and lost
my memories still haunt me
she is my future
not my past

she holds me
she protects me
in her arms I am safe
for every second with her
I give my thanks
and grace

her essence fills me
throughout night and day
I inhale her to my core
she is with me
in every way

I know that I must cherish
her perfection in my eyes
for she is my whole World
my love
for all my life

I KNOW YOU KNOW

---

it fluttered more than a moment
my body through and through
it skipped so many beats
it fluttered because of you

I think of you in my dreams
in the night and in the day
you fill me with life's joy
you are my future's way

the glancing of your touch
the beauty of your smile
shivers run right through me
I wonder all the while

we are at the start
and we will always be
we will spend our lives together
forever you and me

HER SEASONS

---

her laughter shouts aloud
to the simple things she bows
from the birds amongst the trees
to the new spring leaves

through rolling fields of hay
she will dance her merry way
for the beauty she can see
is not revealed to you and me

the wind sweeps in
revealing features never seen
with white toothed smiles
her eyes glinting bright

I see joy that she beholds
walking newly fallen snow
in the crisp winter air
snowflakes falling on her hair

she brings love to my life
with her ever open eyes
she brought warmth to my heart
right from the very start

MAD LOVE

Oh no not again
there's his child within
doing what he shouldn't
a cardinal sin
raising my anger
from reality he hides
I can feel myself raging
deep down inside

"Do as you're told"
I scream in my head
desperately wanting
the frustration to end
it's burning me up
with a knot in my gut
whatever I say
he just won't give it up

Try as I do
when he says
"*me?*"
"YES YOU!"
he melts me inside
with his puppy dog eyes
my shoulders sag down
with a huff
and a sigh

"God you're annoying"
I say through my grin
in my anger I smile
I can't help but love him!

Life

BY THE FIRE

The flames glinted wildly, their reflection in my eyes,
all the laughter and the tears, so much joy in my life.
From the love and the loss, to the beauty of my child,
sometimes mellow, sometimes sad, and yet often it
was wild.

When the flames began to settle, my future found its
way,
in the beauty of her love, we had forever and a day.
Another was still waiting, we lived it to the full,
never parted for a moment, always laughter, never
dull.

The flames flickered gently, it was dusk, no longer
dawn,
in my peace I could reflect, my face was tired and so
worn.
As I came to see my past, with a smile behind my
eyes,
all the joy my life had brought, sometimes tears fell
from my eyes.

Then the flames no longer flickered, they had faded
into ash,
yet forever in my memory, I had lived once in the
past.

THE PASSING OF AGES

Weariness creeps, like vines around an ancient oak,
with an ever tightening grip,
not suffocating, yet gently reminding ~ it is time.

The passing of ages, as the sun begins its last journey,
descending, into the shadows,
to sleep with legends past.

When darkness falls, peace ebbs through the soul,
old lights fade, becoming memories,
entombed, in their own eternal mausoleum.

HOPE ANEW

---

existing in the darkness of eternity
dreams lay amongst the waste
like splintered shards of light
shattered by pain now dulled

to live a life of day
in the confusing haze of chaos
wandering through shrouded mist
as a nomad in the storm

searching for horizons
faint moonbeams in the dusk
glimpsing futures once thought lost
through hazy opaque eyes

the journey can begin
with steps that sometimes stumble
fates compass guides the way
as hope is born anew

ONCE

I grew up there
once
in my memory that now fades
by
the day

was it really so beautiful
I don't recall
now
as a child I felt empty
yet full

is it
as it always was
please remind me
the days past
friends
memories that endure and
last

a sense of peace
I ponder and
I wonder
not sure
but perhaps

no matter
it's simplicity was
to me
my life and all
that I could be

A LIFE LESS ORDINARY

I look at my life
with wonder in my eyes
ordinary they said
with a crooked smile
never be much
a carpenter or cook
the rich and elite
from the outside
take a look

it is all about status
power and wealth
ignore being happy
your sanity
your health
aspire to be more
on their grandest scale
climb up the ladder
do not dare to fail

for many a year
I took their word as all
I fought up the rungs
sometimes to fall
in the maelstrom of life
a career to define
until looking inside
I realised that I hide

then I awakened
my passion was stirred
my life since that day
has passed by in a blur
I now see the qualities
the truth and the lies
that real people matter
others fade and die

I wonder at stars
at flowers and birds
I no longer see them
the cattle in herds
the ants in the cities
clawing their way
to their version of life
each and every day

it is not about status
or power
or wealth
it is about happiness
sanity and health
so when your eyes open
and you see the truth
live your life right
live it well
true to you

MY WINDOW

Shadows pass by, never looking in,
through murky smoked glass, the lights are dim.
Watching the world pass silently by,
sometimes I laugh, and sometimes I cry.

To glimpse the others from deep within,
some tall, some fat, some round, some thin.
I wonder where their haste takes them,
as I peer from within my veiled den.

Afraid to venture to the other side,
where reality exists, and you have to live life.
The fear that rages inside my soul,
is cloaked by my window, growing ever old.

A cocooned world of safety and light,
hidden from life, hidden from sight.

DRIFTING

---

drifting as a feather on the wind
at the mercy of elements
captured by freedom's grasp
~ to roam far

lost souls smile through eyes of delight
whose direction is claimed
by flights of fancy
~ living on a whim

loneliness plunges its blade deep
to awaken the core
back to life's reality
~ eyes open to truth

MORALS

---

do we have morals
every one of us
I look around me
I hear what they say
it runs through my mind
but it doesn't go in
please don't go there
so selfish within

why not be glad
for all that we have
don't lash out at others
they are innocent
it bends my meagre soul
the way that some act
please don't go there
what pleasure is that

don't be bitter
or look back with ire
see the good
it is in you
be true to your soul
do it all right
please don't go there
don't make it a fight

it is innocence hurt
as you lash and you slash
you may feel smug
as your anger boils
but it's you that gets hurt
and the trail that you leave
please don't go there
don't hurt you them or me

THE RIVER

Tiny ripples, small quiet ponds,
stillness lingers, when the days grow long.
Mayflowers bloom in the fresh spring air,
new life begins, when the days become fair.

Receding waters, dried out moss,
revealing a bed, for a year since lost.
At the water's edge, a Kingfisher waits,
for unsuspecting prey, to take its bait.

Swells rise up to the swirling winds,
in the chaotic maelstrom, autumn begins.
Salmon leap the falls and bends,
the time has come, for their journeys end.

Raging torrents of beautiful fury,
show winters might, in all its glory.

ATOP THE WAVES

I look into the circles
of sand beneath my feet
I look into the leaves
in the bottom of my tea

my mind sets out and wanders
as fate plays out its hand
with the rolling of the dice
who knows which way it lands

when I wake up in the morning
what is in store for me
if I step into the world
just what will come to be

is it me who makes the choices
of an ever changing life
or is it fate who can decide
if it is happiness or strife

so I ride atop the waves
for they will not let me stay
I know the joy is in the journey
as they carry me their way

THE FACSIMILE

---

a wisp, a brushed cheek ~ elegant dances
a new street

shivers ~ breathed in
of times past
yet still to begin

once dreamt, deep down ~ no win
no longer a sin

depths ~ once hidden
revealed gently
jealousy ridden

second chances, veiled thoughts ~ scared
laid bare

hope ~ again lingers
far away
grasping fingers

if only ~ the facsimile
no longer lonely

DO I EXIST

---

do I exist
as I rise to the dawn
each new day passes
in waking dreams
what was achieved

do I live
in my simplicity of actions
no thoughts of tomorrow
filling the void
is that enough

what is my purpose
wandering the ether
in a rudderless ship
no compass to guide
should there be more

who will remember
a significance to none
just stroking a pen
leaving musings to read
are my words enough

to exist

RIPPLES OF CHANGE

The calm of liquid life, forever disturbed,
sinking through the depths of an endless pool,
unbalancing the equilibrium, bringing agony in truth
~ waking its core.

Anger, rising from long sunken trenches,
unleashed from its hidden prison,
boiling up through layers of fury, to freedom
~ expelling the waves of change.

Speeding outward, washing all in their path,
bathing them in the inertia of effects,
whose causes ensure inevitable sadness
~ sparing none.

With time, the sands settle once more,
waters calm, to become gentle ripples,
lapping at the shores of the affected
~ now forever altered.

ALONE

---

bathing in the stillness of solitude
a ravenous silence feasts
consuming a new prey
delighting in its conquest

a kingdom is built of thoughts not real
hiding from sanity's truth
as it retreats deeper
into eternal blackness

thoughtful in the silence of one
accepting in hollow relief
of a life once lived
now lost only in the mind

FOR INNOCENCE LOST

---

look at the World with your beautiful innocence
naivety running through veins of rushing blood
so warm and true in the view of all good
hidden from truth as a child in a mother's arms
to the horrors awaiting those stepping out of the
shadows

laughter in the dusk of the ever fading sun
as the evening song retreats for the end of days
bringing a new dawn where all before shatters
with the ruthlessness of harsh reality
splintered shards piercing previously known truths
ripping through the fabric of a life lived well
taking innocence away to an ever guarded cell

weep for that lost as a life turns inside never again
revealed
tears for a soul taken hostage by pain ever intended
actions and reactions inextricably chained together
rolling uncontrollably from the psyche of damage
causes not known discarded by their irrelevance
to effects ever felt as their echoes reach far in time
no hiding for one touched by such sadness

cycles repeat like the rising sun now tainted
blood red in the sky haunting only one
shed your tears at that lost never again to be found
life changed eternally searching for peace in vain
burdened by the carnage of foul deeds inflicted
dark seeds spreading like a plague on the land
bathing in the misery of their taunting at what has
been done

weep now for all that is gone

weep now for innocence lost

BORROWED TIME

---

carelessly free as the new sun rising
dancing on the shimmering clouds
time ticks by on the hands of pleasure
~ a tacit contract signed

teasing the day through nights of play
feeding flesh to extract life's essence
savouring the last drops taste
~ hungry for more

ignorant to the edge of realisation
a precipice smiling with gorging eyes
patiently awaiting its dues
~ collecting its profit

THE PATH

---

the wind blows
the river flows
which way will it turn
our lives play out
before our eyes
a lesson never learned

we have our plan
we know the way
of this we can be sure
but then it kinks
meanders and jinks
its path is never pure

sometimes we hold
our heads up high
so happy and so proud
yet other times
we shed our tears
we cry so hard and loud

such zest for life
when we set out
don't let it grind you down
live each day
as if the last
with a smile and not a frown

some face the journey
filled with dread
they cannot see a light
yet others see it shining there
so brilliant
strong and bright

some see no path
and live in fear
they are frozen
still and numb
others see no path ahead
but smile at what may come

your road through life
is still not clear
the path is not yet made
so when life takes you
by surprise
you should not feel afraid

for all the past
is done and gone
your memories vivid and clear
your life is now
your future bright
now live it without fear

DECEPTION

---

what should have been
loyalty
a future
harmony
together

feelings erupt within
anger
the agony
disappointment
betrayal

the foundations crumble
emptiness
a void
all is lost
futures bent

what have you done
soul crushing
infidelity
a lie
deception

THE TEARS OF ANGELS

shimmering silver blades
dancing in the moonlight
the crystal prisms fall
like divine rapiers
descending their throne
to the mortal world

filled with heavens aura
simplicity is their beauty
a purity of purpose
washing over the land
cleansing the sins
to bring absolution

seeds of life raise
anew from the waste
their hunger for more
as new shoots bloom
impatient again to bathe
in the tears of angels

EMERGENCE

---

so bright
for long sleeping eyes
slowly
so slowly opening
startling beauty revealed
a new virgin born

daylight floods in waves
the womb now departed
safe warmth lost
replaced
by the crisp spring chill

smells explode in colour
all confusion is momentary
discovery begins anew
familiarity
not yet bred

sounds resonate in dulled ears
soft songs noticed
yet distant
sharp fear stabs
through shrill cries
subsiding
in the safety of kin

mothers milk fills hungry mouths
bringing serene comfort
feeding life ahead
guiding
the way through

faltering steps begin
as the new day
from the dawn of birth
new life awakens
emerging
into its journey

WHAT DO YOU SEE

---

a shallow pond
mere ripples of nothingness
lifeless
empty
devoid of all

no thoughts
regurgitating others
false smiles
vain guile

stones thrown in
they cannot sink
light penetrates
depths seen

what do you see ~ so shallow ~ me

a vast ocean
waves crash on beaches
teaming with life
naive nature

minds complex
raging whirls
too fast
colours flash

no sense made
too much there
murky darkness
many needs

what do you see ~ too deep ~ me

IT IS BETTER TO HIDE

---

darkness not penetrated
your mask secure
veiled from truth and fragility
with confidence high
standing tall
feeling strong
as you hide

the mask comes off in solitude
your castle is safe
none can get through
do not look in the mirror
all revealed
even inside
you must hide

glance for a moment
what will be seen
too real
who is there
so weak I see not recognised
go now run
please hide

why are you here in my mind
I do not know you
go
is that me
do not let it be
I will slip back behind
it is better to hide

THE SOLITUDE OF SELF

Living life, in words of cryptic meaning,
in plain sight to all ~ yet understood by few.
Defining that pain which shapes the future,
consumed with what is gone.

Tortured, feeding the soul fresh inspiration,
whose agony delivers genius to the page,
with slashes of the pen,
dispelling the past.

Peace is found in the solitude of self,
where history remains, forever hidden,
for the safety of sanity,
easing the burden.

AWAKENING

---

sun beams meander lazily over the horizon
with no urgency for the inevitability of creeping time
relentlessly enlightening the path ahead

moist dew is inhaled into all being
with the first waking breaths
infusing life's blood as the food of the soul

morning songs pierce the dawn of red mist haze
dancing through the still dulled senses
awakening to the birth of a new day

LIFE IN COLOUR

---

dark not light
grey not bright
is life like that
all of the time

some see it black
some see it white
some with the grey
bringing the night

there are doers and thinkers
nearly men
always the same
throughout all of your friends

I would have and could have
are what they say
life slipped by them
in every way

yet some see the colours
wonderful and bright
they are vibrant and glowing
with life and light

a depth so deep
that you cannot see
but they can dream
in wonder and believe

their eyes are open
so wide and true
for they are the ones
who bring life not you

I dare you to join them
set yourself free
are your eyes open
be alive like me

A POET'S LIFE

---

why am I still here
in my darkened room
immersed in the shadows
black tearing through
like a rapier passing by
missing me

that it should elude me for so long
time idles its way
to what seems like eternity
never loosening its grip
on my every tortured
waking moment

why won't it come to me
so needed but lost
not yet found
like the days when I search for it
the thing that makes me
defining my purpose

will it be soon
anticipation rising high
taking me into seduction
to draw me ever closer
mocking me through crooked lips
with taunting smile

now it's too late
thoughts are flooding out
a jumbled mass
to be re-ordered for sanity
and satiate my lust
for the fantasy to finish
with words finally penned

SPRING TIME

---

at the beginning
sleep was still here
woken from slumber
an edge of fear

hunger upon them
hunters and prey
to fight for their food
or to run away

order returned
the grass and the blossom
not long from now
a new mothers bosom

firstly to forage
food then a mate
for so long asleep
now finally awake

who will be chosen
the strongest of all
the weak are forgotten
they stumble and fall

new life is born
cycles repeated
eternity continues
never defeated

the sun rises higher
days growing longer
adolescence approaches
bodies get stronger

a new dawn is over
the clouds are all cleared
for now it is over
summer time is here

WHEN SHE RETURNS

A faint touch brushes, and lingers,
the memory of her soft, caressing fingers.
A gentle shiver courses through me,
I turn to look, yet cannot see.

My senses deceived, her scent drifts by,
I search for her, I do not know why.
For now I must endure the pain,
to hope once more, will be in vain.

So long since gone, that she now fades,
her delicate colours, lost in shade.
For now I wait in agony,
for the day that she comes back to me.

Not long now, holding back my fears.
daring to look, my relief in tears.

ACKNOWLEDGEMENTS

David Johnson of maxblackphotos: for the stunning photograph used as the book cover which, to me, perfectly represents The Lonely Tree. The photograph was taken at Hadrian's Wall and perfectly encapsulates the mood of rustic poetry.

The poem Starlight Sanctuary is inspired by the wonderful children's book, The Starlight Sailor, written and illustrated by the talented artist, Jackie Morris. It happened that I took my family to Pembrokeshire and stayed in a Mongolian yurt at Trellyn Woodland Camping. The canvass of the yurt had been beautifully hand decorated by Jackie with characters from her book ~ mermaids, dolphins and unicorns. After the most inspiring of weeks, it seemed appropriate to try and put into words the spirit of her book, combined with my feelings about the experiences I had.

www.ingramcontent.com/pod-product-compliance
Lightning Source LLC
Chambersburg PA
CBHW050956050726
47592CB00007B/2598